1
2
3
4
5
6
7
8
9
0
11
2
3
4
5
6
7
8
9
0

1

Color the picture.

2 =  blue   6 = green   10 = red

4 = yellow   8 = black   12 = orange

2

Circle the correct number.

4 5 8

1 2 3

7 8 10

10 12 13

3

First connect the black dots.
Then connect the gray dots.

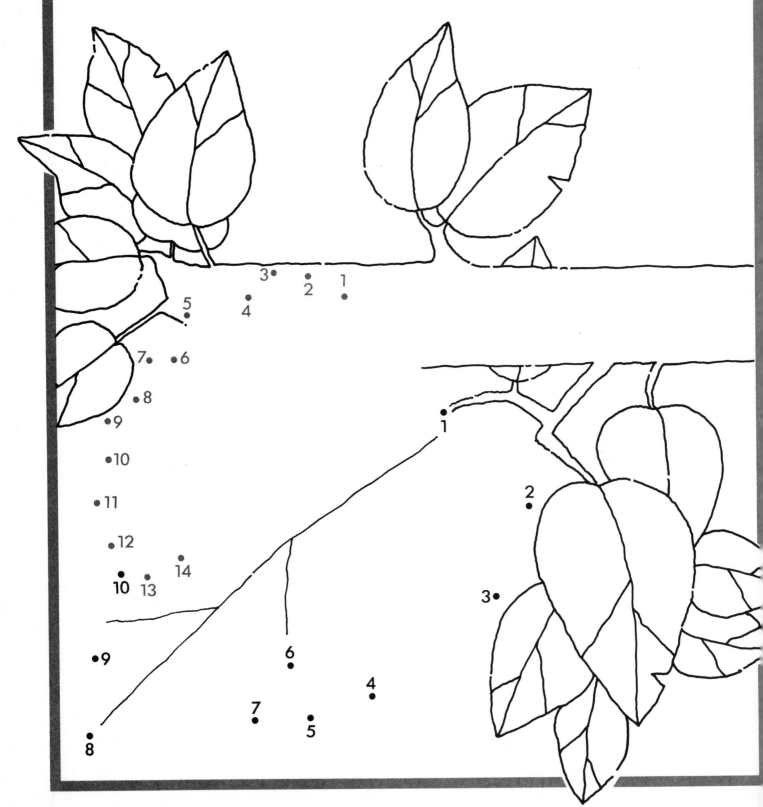

4

Draw a line from each group of things
to the number that goes with it.

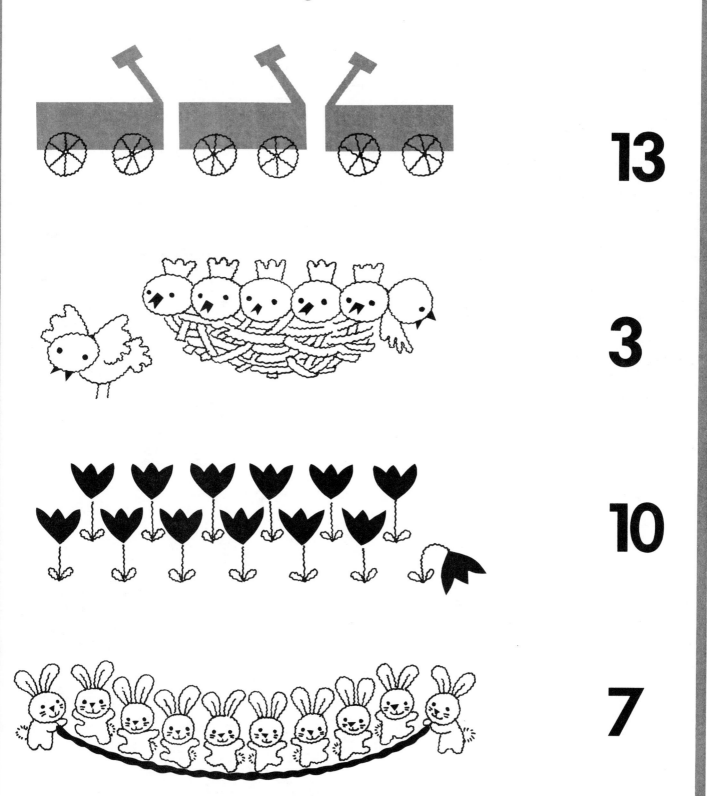

13

3

10

7

Find the two hidden numbers.
Color the hidden numbers.

Color the picture.

1 = purple   5 = orange   9 = green
3 = yellow   7 = blue   11 = brown

How many ? _____

How many ? _____

How many ? _____

How many things are there?
Write the correct number next to each picture.

_____
- - - - - - - - -
_____

_____
- - - - - - - - -
_____

_____
- - - - - - - - -
_____

_____
- - - - - - - - -
_____

_____
- - - - - - - - -
_____

How many  ? _____

How many ? _____

How many HONEY ? _____

Draw a line from each word
to the number that goes with it.

three	9
twenty	3
nine	12
twelve	10
ten	20

Find the three hidden numbers.
Color the hidden numbers.

How many things are there?
Write the correct number next to each picture.

Draw a line from each group of things to the number that goes with it.

15   **1**   **7**   **18**   **2**

Circle the correct number.

6 8 5

8 7 9

12 13 11

5 4 6

How many  ? _ _ _ _ _   How many

How many ? _ _ _ _ _   How many

How many ? _ _ _ _ _   How many

16

17

Draw a line from each group of things to the number that goes with it.

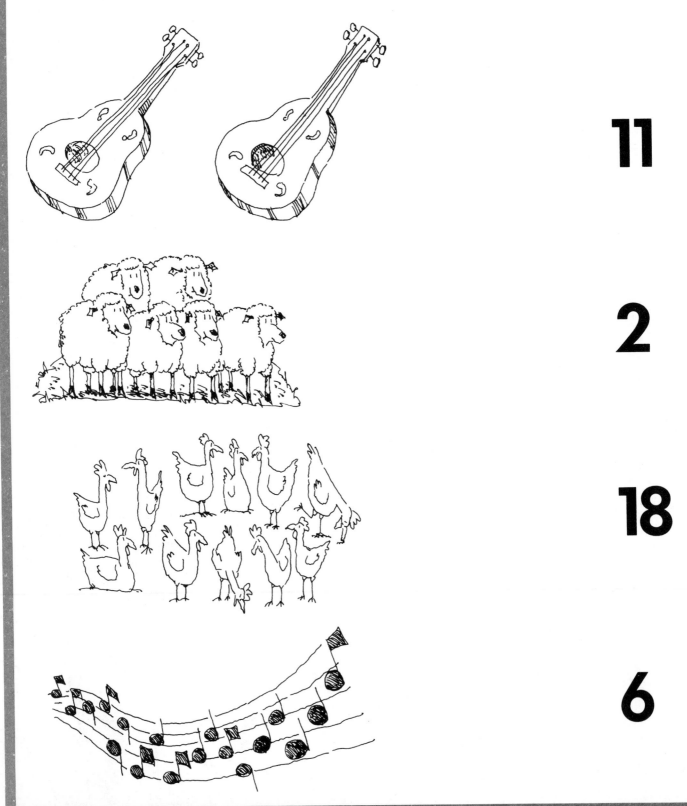

11

2

18

6

Find the two hidden numbers.
Color the numbers.

Look at the number each caterpillar is holding.
One caterpillar has a **wrong** number!
Circle the caterpillar that has the **wrong** number.

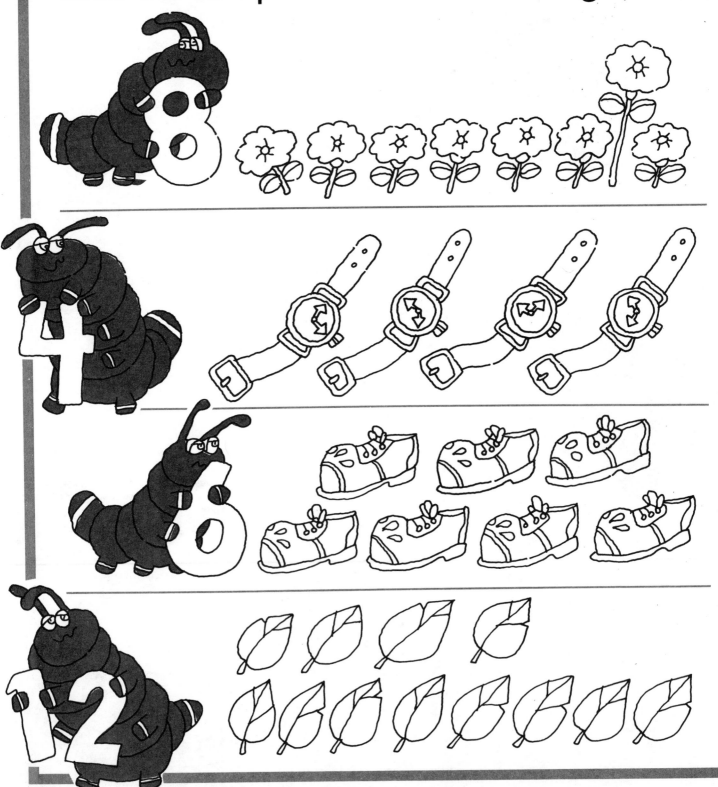

First connect the black dots.
Then connect the gray dots.

Draw a line from each word
to the number that goes with it.

seven   **11**

eight   **8**

four   **6**

eleven   **7**

six   **4**

Draw a line from each group of things to the number that goes with it.

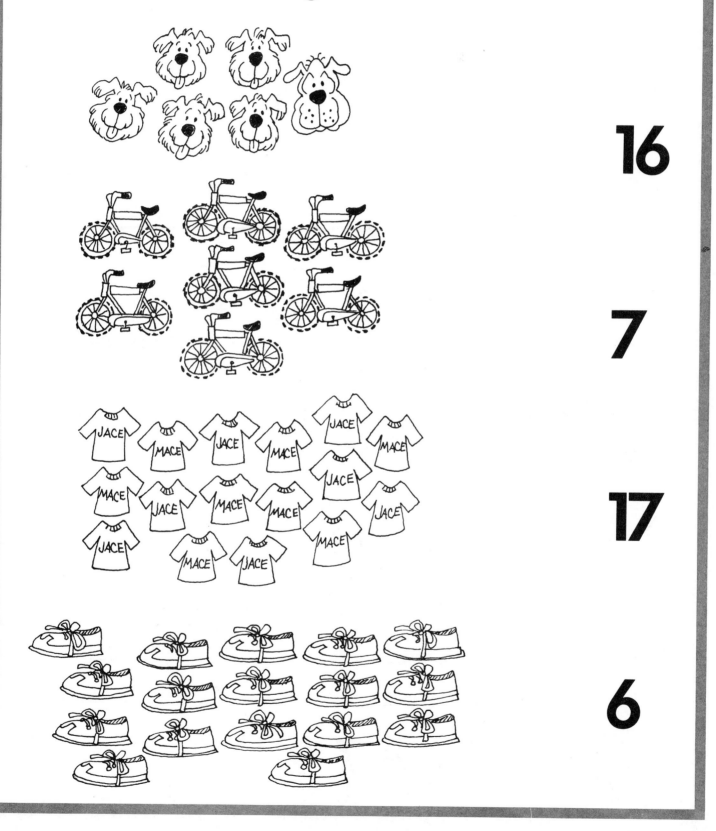

16

7

17

6

Circle the correct number.

9 10 11

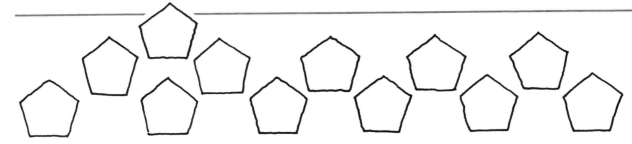

14 13 12

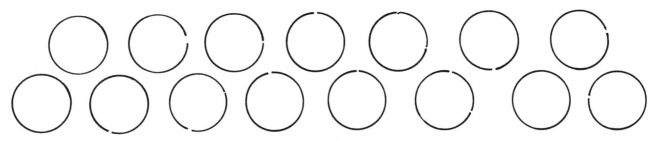

13 14 15

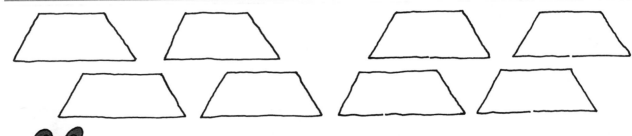

8 7 9

24

First connect the gray dots.
Then connect the black dots.

Look at the number each turtle is holding.
One of the turtles is holding a **wrong** number!
Circle the turtle that has the **wrong** number.

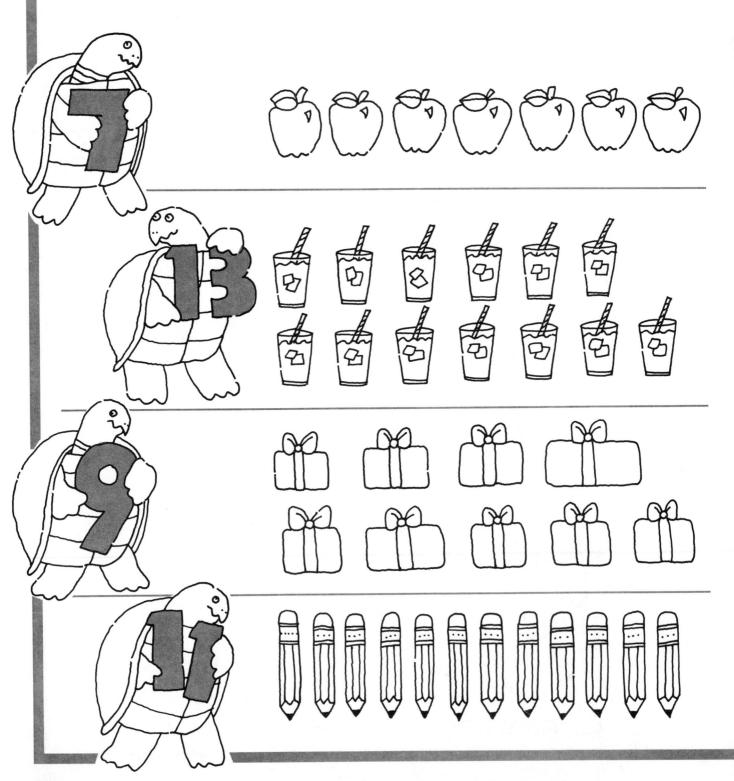

Color the picture.

11 = 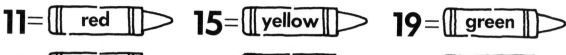 red 15 = yellow 19 = green

13 = blue 17 = black 20 = purple

First connect the gray dots.
Then connect the black dots.

Find the two hidden numbers.
Color the hidden numbers.

How many things are there?
Write the correct number next to each picture.

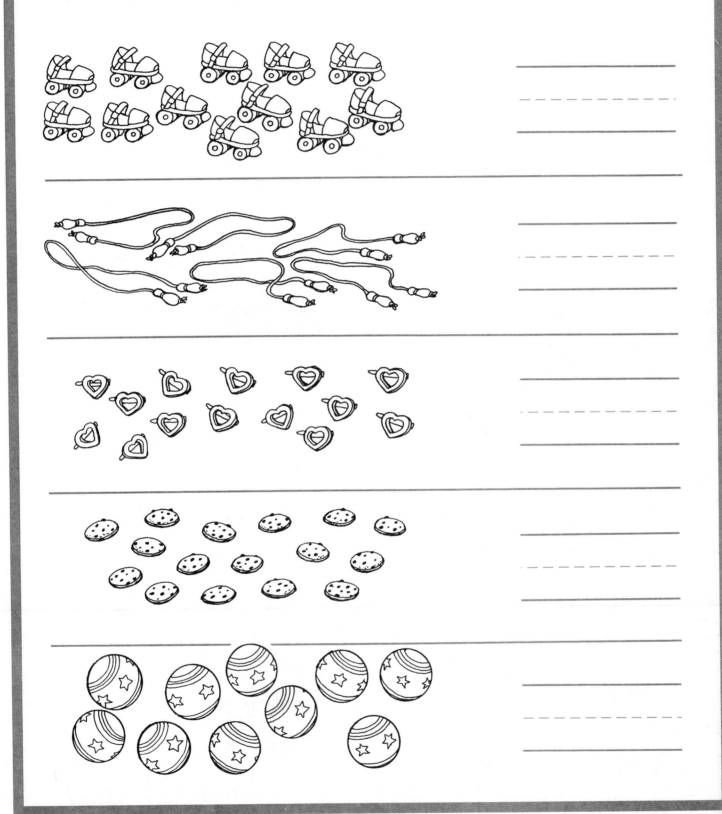

How many ⬭ ? ------
How many ⬜ ? ------
How many △ ? ------

Color the picture.

10 = orange   14 = red   18 = blue

12 = green   16 = yellow   20 = black

0250